FIT OVER FORTY

A CONCISE GUIDE TO FITNESS AND LIVING WELL

TRAY T. LARSON

CONTENTS

INTRODUCTION: THE IMPORTANCE OF FITNESS AFTER FORTY

As we age, our bodies require more attention and care to maintain the quality of life we desire. Aging, however, should not be viewed as an inevitable decline but as an opportunity to redefine our relationship with our self. Being fit after forty is not just a way to maintain our health but is a cornerstone for living a full, rich life.

A New Chapter in Health

Entering our fifth decade brings with it changes that underscore the importance of fitness. Our metabolism slows, muscle mass naturally decreases, and the risks for certain health conditions, such as cardiovascular disease and type 2 diabetes, increase. However, these challenges provide catalysts for adopting more proactive approaches to physical wellbeing.

The Multifaceted Benefits of Fitness

Developing and maintaining our fitness after forty is a worthwhile challenge, offering benefits that extend far beyond physical health:

- **Physical Resilience:** Regular exercise helps counteract the loss of muscle mass and bone density, improving strength, flexibility, and balance, making daily activities easier and reducing the risk of falls.
- **Chronic Disease Prevention:** An active lifestyle plays a crucial role in preventing and managing chronic diseases, including heart disease, diabetes, and certain types of cancer.
- **Mental Health:** Physical activity is a powerful mood booster, reducing symptoms of anxiety and depression, and enhancing cognitive function, which is particularly important as we age.

- **Longevity and Quality of Life:** Staying fit over forty can add years to your life and, more importantly, life to your years, enabling you to engage more fully in activities you enjoy and spend quality time with loved ones.

Embracing a Holistic Approach

Fitness after forty is not just about hitting the gym or counting steps; it's about embracing a holistic approach that integrates physical activity, proper nutrition, adequate rest, and stress management. This balanced approach ensures that the body, mind, and spirit are all nurtured, leading to a more fulfilling and vibrant life.

The Path Forward

Committing to fitness over forty is not about recapturing your youth—although it certainly can help you feel younger—but about building a strong foundation for the future. This fitness journey is about setting achievable goals, celebrating progress, and adapting to the body's changing needs.

This guidebook is your companion on this journey, offering insights, strategies, and motivation to help you navigate the path to fitness and wellbeing for your whole life, after forty and beyond.

PART I

UNDERSTANDING THE AGING PROCESS AND GETTING STARTED

1
UNDERSTANDING THE AGING BODY

As we journey beyond our forties, our bodies undergo a series of natural transformations that influence our physical capabilities and fitness needs. Recognizing and understanding these changes are pivotal in crafting a fitness approach that is not only effective but also sustainable and kind to our evolving selves.

Physiological Changes

Several key physiological changes occur as we age, each impacting our approach to fitness and overall wellbeing:

- **Muscle Mass and Strength:** One of the

most notable changes is the gradual loss of muscle mass and strength, a process known as sarcopenia. This can begin as early as our thirties and accelerates with each passing decade. Maintaining muscle mass is crucial for metabolic health, physical stability, and everyday functional abilities.

- **Metabolic Adjustments:** Our metabolism naturally slows down, affecting how our bodies process calories and nutrients. This change necessitates a more mindful approach to nutrition and exercise to manage weight and energy levels effectively.
- **Bone Density:** The density of our bones may decrease over time, increasing the risk of osteoporosis and fractures. Weight-bearing and resistance exercises become essential components of a fitness regimen to support bone health.
- **Joint Health:** The wear and tear on our joints become more pronounced, potentially leading to discomfort and conditions like osteoarthritis. Incorporating low-impact exercises and flexibility training can help preserve joint function and alleviate pain.
- **Cardiovascular and Respiratory Efficiency:** There may be changes in cardiovascular and respiratory efficiency, making it crucial to include

heart-healthy aerobic activities in our fitness routines while being mindful of our individual limits.

Adaptation and Awareness

Understanding these changes is not about resigning ourselves to a fate of decline but about adapting our fitness strategies to work harmoniously with our bodies. It's about:

- **Listening to Our Bodies:** Paying close attention to how our bodies respond to different types of exercise and adjusting accordingly.
- **Seeking Balance:** Finding the right mix of cardiovascular, strength, flexibility, and balance training to address the body's changing needs.
- **Prioritizing Recovery:** Emphasizing rest and recovery, recognizing that our bodies might need more time to heal and regenerate after physical activities.

A Proactive Approach

. . .

Armed with this understanding, we can proactively address the changes associated with aging, turning potential challenges into opportunities for growth and revitalization. This first section of the guidebook aims to empower you with the knowledge to make informed decisions about your fitness journey, embracing the aging process with grace and vigor.

2

GETTING STARTED

Setting Realistic Goals

Embarking on your fitness journey over forty begins with setting realistic, achievable goals. This initial step is not just about aspiration; it's about creating a clear, attainable roadmap that respects your current lifestyle, health status, and personal commitments. Here's how to approach goal-setting effectively:

Understand Your Starting Point

Before setting your sights on where you want to go, it's essential to understand where you currently stand. Consider factors such as:

• **Current Fitness Level:** Assess your current state of physical fitness honestly. Have you been active regularly, or are you looking to start exercising after a hiatus?

• **Health Considerations:** Take into account any existing health issues or concerns that might influence your fitness regimen. Consulting with healthcare professionals can provide valuable insights and guidelines.

Define Clear, Specific Goals

Vague aspirations like "get fit" or "lose weight" lack the clarity needed for actionable steps. Instead, define specific goals such as:

• **Performance Goals:** Setting targets like walking a certain distance without stopping, completing a set of strength exercises, or gradually increasing workout duration can be highly motivating.

• **Health Metrics:** Goals related to improving health markers, such as lowering blood pressure, achieving a healthier body composition, or enhancing mobility and balance, can also be impactful.

. . .

Embrace the S.M.A.R.T. Criteria

Ensuring your goals are Specific, Measurable, Achievable, Relevant, and Time-bound (S.M.A.R.T.) can significantly increase your chances of success:

- **Specific:** Clearly define what you want to achieve.
- **Measurable:** Ensure your goal can be tracked and assessed.
- **Achievable:** Your goal should be challenging yet attainable, considering your current capabilities.
- **Relevant:** Your goal should align with your personal values and long-term objectives.
- **Time-bound:** Set a realistic timeline for achieving your goal.

Consider Short-Term and Long-Term Goals

While long-term goals provide a vision for what you want to achieve, short-term goals act as milestones along the way. For instance, if your long-term goal is to complete a 10K run, a short-term goal might be to jog without stopping for 20 minutes.

Flexibility Is Key

Life over forty can be unpredictable, with numerous demands on your time, various responsibilities, and many unexpected changes. Your goals should have the flexibility to adapt to life's ebbs and flows without causing frustration or creating a sense of failure.

Celebrate Every Achievement

Recognize and celebrate each milestone, no matter how small. This positive reinforcement builds momentum and keeps you motivated throughout your fitness journey.

. . .

Setting realistic goals is the cornerstone of embarking on a successful fitness journey over forty, providing direction, motivation, and a sense of achievement.

3

ASSESSMENT AND BASELINE

Before embarking on any fitness journey, particularly after the age of forty, it's essential to establish a clear, objective baseline of your current physical health and fitness level. This initial assessment will serve as a foundation for setting realistic goals, designing an effective fitness plan, and measuring progress over time.

Consult with Healthcare Professionals

- **Medical Check-Up:** A comprehensive medical examination can uncover any underlying health conditions that may affect your fitness routine. It's particularly important to assess heart health, blood pressure, and any risk factors for chronic diseases.

- **Fitness Assessment with a Professional:** Consider working with a certified fitness trainer or physiotherapist for an in-depth fitness assessment. This can include evaluating your cardiovascular fitness, muscular strength and endurance, flexibility, and body composition.

Self-Assessment Tools

- **Basic Fitness Tests:** Simple tests can be done at home to assess aspects of your fitness. For example, the number of push-ups you can do without stopping, how long you can hold a plank, or how far you can walk or run in a set time.
- **Tracking Daily Activity Levels:** Utilizing a pedometer or a smartwatch to track your daily steps and active minutes can provide insights into your current activity level.

Establishing a Baseline

. . .

• **Record Initial Measurements:** Document key metrics from your assessments, such as weight, body measurements, results from fitness tests, and any relevant health indicators (e.g., cholesterol levels, blood pressure).

• **Personal Fitness Journal:** Consider starting a fitness journal or digital log to record your baseline measurements, daily activity, workouts, and how you feel physically and mentally. This record will be invaluable for tracking your progress and adjusting your plan as needed.

Setting the Stage for Personalized Goals

With a clear understanding of your starting point, you can set personalized, realistic fitness goals. The baseline assessment ensures that these goals are tailored to your current abilities, health status, and lifestyle, making them more attainable and meaningful.

. . .

Re-assessment and Adaptation

- **Plan for Regular Check-Ins:** Set intervals for re-assessing your fitness level and health metrics, such as every 3 to 6 months. This will help you gauge your progress, celebrate improvements, and adjust your goals and fitness plan as needed.

Establishing a solid assessment and baseline is not just about numbers; it's about gaining insights into your health and fitness, setting the stage for a journey that is both challenging and achievable. This thoughtful approach ensures that your fitness plan over forty is built on a foundation of self-awareness and personalized goals.

Having established your baseline, you're now in a strong position to embark on your fitness journey with clarity and confidence.

4

MINDSET AND MOTIVATION

Starting your fitness journey over forty presents unique challenges and opportunities. Cultivating a positive mindset and maintaining motivation are key to navigating this path successfully. Here's how you can fortify your mental resilience and stay driven:

Cultivating a Growth Mindset

- **Embrace Learning:** View your fitness journey as an opportunity to learn new skills, understand your body better, and explore what makes you feel most vibrant and alive.

• **Resilience in the Face of Setbacks:** Accept that setbacks are part of the journey. What matters most is your ability to bounce back and learn from these experiences.

• **Celebrate Small Wins:** Every step forward, no matter how small, is progress. Acknowledge and celebrate these achievements to reinforce positive behavior and outcomes.

Motivation Strategies

• **Find Your 'Why':** Deeply reflect on the reasons behind your decision to pursue fitness. Whether it's improving your health to enjoy more activities with your family, feeling more energetic, or managing stress better, your 'why' is a powerful motivator that can keep you pushing forward even on tough days.

• **Set Inspirational Goals:** Beyond the physical goals, set aspirations that inspire you on a personal level. This could be participating in a charity walk, mastering a new sport, or achieving a lifelong dream of hiking a famous trail.

• **Visualize Success:** Regularly visualize yourself achieving your goals. Imagine how you will feel and the positive changes it will bring to your life. This visualization can be a strong motivator, especially on days when your energy or commitment wanes.

Building a Support System

• **Seek Like-Minded Individuals:** Joining a group or community, whether it's a local walking club, a gym class, or an online fitness community, can provide encouragement, accountability, and a sense of belonging.

• **Involve Your Family and Friends:** Share your fitness goals with your loved ones. They can offer support, join you in your activities, and celebrate your milestones, making the journey more enjoyable and meaningful.

Managing Expectations

. . .

- **Patience is Key:** Understand that progress, especially after forty, might be slower than expected. Physical changes and improvements in fitness levels take time and consistent effort.
- **Adaptability:** Be willing to adapt your goals and strategies as you progress. What works at the beginning may need to be adjusted as you become fitter, encounter plateaus, or face life changes.

Celebrating the Journey

- **Enjoy the Process:** Instead of fixating solely on the end goals, find joy in the daily activities, the feeling of being active, and the positive changes in your lifestyle and mindset.
- **Reflective Practice:** Regular reflection on your journey, the hurdles you've overcome, and the knowledge you've gained can provide a profound sense of accomplishment and motivation to continue.

Fostering a positive mindset and keeping motivation high are as crucial as the physical aspects of your fitness journey. They are the driving forces that will keep you committed, help you overcome challenges, and ultimately lead to lasting change and fulfillment.

PART II

COMPONENTS OF FITNESS

5

COMPONENTS OF FITNESS: STRENGTH TRAINING

Strength training, often associated with weights and gyms, is far more than just building muscle mass; it's a key component in maintaining functional fitness, increasing metabolic health, encouraging longevity, and fostering independence as we age. After forty, incorporating strength training into your fitness regimen becomes increasingly important due to the natural decline in muscle strength and mass, known as sarcopenia.

Understanding the Benefits

. . .

- **Counteracts Muscle Loss:** Regular strength training helps mitigate the effects of sarcopenia, maintaining or even increasing muscle mass and strength.
- **Boosts Metabolic Rate:** Muscle tissue burns more calories than fat, even at rest. By increasing muscle mass, you can enhance your metabolic rate, aiding in weight management.
- **Enhances Bone Density:** Strength training is beneficial for bone health, reducing the risk of osteoporosis by stimulating bone growth and increasing bone density.
- **Improves Functional Fitness:** Building strength enhances your ability to perform everyday activities, from carrying groceries to climbing stairs, with ease and less risk of injury.
- **Supports Joint Health:** Proper strength training can alleviate stress on joints by building the muscles around them, providing better support and reducing the risk of joint issues.

Getting Started

. . .

- **Consultation with Professionals:** Before starting any strength training program, especially if you're new to exercise or have existing health concerns, consulting with a fitness professional or healthcare provider is advisable. They can help design a program tailored to your needs and abilities.
- **Bodyweight Exercises:** Start with exercises that use your body weight, such as push-ups, squats, and lunges, to build foundational strength without the need for equipment.
- **Progression to Weights:** Gradually incorporate free weights, resistance bands, or weight machines into your routine, focusing on proper form and technique to prevent injuries.
- **Frequency and Repetitions:** Aim for 2 to 3 strength training sessions per week, allowing for rest days in between. Start with lighter weights or fewer repetitions, gradually increasing as your strength improves.

Balancing Intensity and Safety

. . .

• **Listen to Your Body:** Pay attention to how your body responds during and after workouts. Some soreness is normal, but sharp pain or discomfort is a sign to stop and reassess.

• **Rest and Recovery:** Adequate rest between sessions is crucial for muscle recovery and growth. Ensure you're allowing enough time for your muscles to heal and strengthen.

• **Variety in Exercises:** Regularly changing your strength training routine can prevent boredom, challenge different muscle groups, and reduce the risk of overuse injuries.

Long-Term Commitment

Strength training is not a quick fix but a lifelong commitment to maintaining your physical health and vitality. Setting incremental goals, celebrating progress, and adapting your routine as you age will keep strength training an enjoyable and integral part of your fitness journey.

. . .

Strength training after forty is a powerful tool for enhancing overall health, functional abilities, and quality of life. With the right approach, it can be safely and effectively incorporated into your fitness routine, providing a strong foundation for a healthy, active future.

6

COMPONENTS OF FITNESS: CARDIOVASCULAR HEALTH

Cardiovascular exercise, often referred to as cardio, encompasses any activity that increases your heart rate and respiratory rate, challenging your heart and lung capacity. For individuals over forty, maintaining cardiovascular health is paramount, not only for fitness but also for reducing the risk of heart disease, stroke, and other conditions associated with aging.

The Benefits of Cardiovascular Exercise

- **Enhanced Heart Health:** Regular cardio helps strengthen the heart muscle, improving its ability to pump blood more efficiently throughout the body.

• **Improved Metabolic Function:** Cardio exercise can help regulate blood sugar levels, manage blood pressure, and decrease LDL cholesterol (the "bad" cholesterol), contributing to overall metabolic health.

• **Increased Lung Capacity:** Engaging in aerobic activities can enhance the efficiency of your lungs, ensuring that your body's tissues receive an ample supply of oxygen.

• **Weight Management:** Cardiovascular exercise is effective in burning calories, aiding in weight management and reducing the risk of obesity-related health issues.

• **Mood and Cognitive Benefits:** Aerobic exercise releases endorphins, natural mood lifters, and has been linked to improved memory, cognitive function, and reduced risk of depression.

Getting Started with Cardio

• **Find Activities You Enjoy:** The key to consistency is enjoyment. Activities such as brisk walking, cycling, swimming, dancing, or group fitness classes can make cardiovascular exercise both effective and enjoyable.

• **Intensity and Duration:** Start with moderate-intensity activities, where you can talk but not sing during the activity, for at least 150 minutes per week, as recommended by health organizations. Alternatively, 75 minutes of vigorous-intensity activity, where talking becomes difficult, can suffice.

• **Incorporate Interval Training:** High-Intensity Interval Training (HIIT) can be a time-efficient way to improve cardiovascular health, alternating short bursts of high-intensity exercise with recovery periods. Ensure to proceed with caution and consult a professional if you're new to HIIT.

Monitoring Your Heart Rate

• **Understanding Target Heart Rate:** Knowing your target heart rate zone can help you exercise at an intensity that is safe and effective. Generally, aim for 50% to 70% of your maximum heart rate for moderate-intensity activities and 70% to 85% for vigorous activities.

- **Use of Technology:** Fitness trackers and heart rate monitors can be valuable tools in ensuring you're working within your target heart rate zone, allowing for adjustments as needed for optimal benefits.

Adapting to Your Needs

- **Low-Impact Options:** For individuals with joint concerns or other physical limitations, low-impact exercises like swimming, cycling, rowing, or using an elliptical machine can provide cardiovascular benefits without excessive strain on the body.
- **Listen to Your Body:** As always, it's essential to listen to your body and adjust the intensity, duration, and type of cardio to suit your current fitness level and health status.

Building a Sustainable Routine

. . .

- **Gradual Progression:** Gradually increase the duration, frequency, and intensity of your cardio workouts to continue challenging your cardiovascular system without overdoing it.
- **Mix It Up:** Incorporating a variety of cardio exercises can keep your routine exciting and work different muscle groups, enhancing overall fitness and preventing boredom.

Maintaining cardiovascular health is a cornerstone of fitness, especially as we age. With the right approach, cardiovascular exercise can be a safe, enjoyable, and integral part of your fitness regimen, offering numerous benefits for your heart, body, and mind.

7

COMPONENTS OF FITNESS: FLEXIBILITY AND BALANCE

Flexibility and balance are key components of a well-rounded fitness regimen, particularly as we age. Flexibility involves the ability of your muscles and joints to move through their full range of motion, while balance is the ability to maintain your body's center of gravity within its base of support. Both become increasingly important after forty, as flexibility tends to decrease and balance can become compromised with age, affecting mobility and increasing the risk of falls.

The Importance of Flexibility and Balance

- **Injury Prevention:** Improved flexibility and

balance can help prevent falls and muscle strains, reducing the risk of injury.

- **Reduced Pain and Stiffness:** Regular flexibility exercises can alleviate muscle tightness and joint pain, often associated with aging and sedentary lifestyles.
- **Improved Posture and Alignment:** Stretching and balance exercises help correct poor posture and alignment, which can alleviate back and neck pain.
- **Enhanced Daily Functioning:** Flexibility and balance are critical for everyday activities, such as reaching, bending, and walking, ensuring independence and quality of life.

Incorporating Flexibility Exercises

- **Dynamic Stretching:** Begin your workout sessions with dynamic stretches to warm up the muscles and prepare them for activity. Examples include leg swings, arm circles, and gentle torso twists.
- **Static Stretching:** Conclude your workouts with static stretching, where you hold a stretch for 20-

30 seconds, to improve flexibility. Focus on major muscle groups such as the hamstrings, quads, shoulders, and lower back.

- **Yoga and Pilates:** These disciplines are excellent for enhancing flexibility, balance, and core strength, offering routines that can be adapted to various fitness levels.

Building Better Balance

- **Balance-Specific Exercises:** Incorporate exercises that challenge your balance into your routine, such as standing on one foot, walking heel-to-toe, or using balance equipment like a BOSU ball or stability board.
- **Strength Training:** Strengthening the muscles of your legs and core (abdominals, lower back, hips) can significantly improve your balance. Exercises like squats, lunges, and planks are beneficial.
- **Tai Chi:** This gentle form of martial arts is renowned for its balance-improving qualities, emphasizing slow, controlled movements and deep breathing.

. . .

Safety and Progression

- **Start Slowly:** If you're new to flexibility and balance training, start slowly and gradually increase the complexity and duration of your exercises.
- **Use Support:** Initially, use a chair, wall, or another stable object for support when practicing balance exercises, gradually reducing reliance as your balance improves.
- **Consistency is Key:** Incorporate flexibility and balance exercises into your routine several times a week for the best results.

Listening to Your Body

- **Avoid Overstretching:** While it's important to challenge your muscles, never stretch to the point of pain. Gentle tension in the muscle is sufficient.
- **Mindful Movement:** Pay attention to your body's cues during balance and flexibility exercises. If an exercise feels unsafe or causes discomfort, adjust your approach or seek professional guidance.

. . .

Enhancing flexibility and balance is not only about improving your physical fitness; it's about enriching your quality of life by maintaining your mobility, independence, and ability to engage in the activities you love.

8

COMPONENTS OF FITNESS: CORE STABILITY

The core, often misunderstood as just the abdominal muscles, encompasses the entire trunk, including the back, sides, pelvic floor, and the muscles around the abdomen. Core stability refers to the ability of these muscles to support the spine and pelvis, maintain good posture, and ensure efficient movement patterns. For individuals over forty, strengthening the core is vital for maintaining balance, preventing lower back pain, and enhancing overall physical performance.

The Role of Core Stability

- **Injury Prevention:** A strong core supports the

spine, reducing the strain on the back and lowering the risk of back injuries.

- **Improved Posture and Alignment:** Core strength helps maintain proper posture, which can alleviate common issues like lower back and neck pain.
- **Enhanced Balance and Stability:** The core acts as the body's center of gravity. Strengthening it enhances your balance, crucial for preventing falls and improving performance in physical activities.
- **Better Functional Movements:** Daily activities, from lifting groceries to getting out of a chair, rely on core strength. A stable core makes these movements more efficient and less effortful.

Strengthening the Core

- **Engage in Core-Specific Exercises:** Incorporate exercises that target the various core muscles, such as planks, bridges, abdominal crunches, and leg raises. These exercises can be modified to suit all fitness levels.
- **Integrate Core Work into Other Exercises:** Many strength training and aerobic exercises

also engage the core. Focus on maintaining good form and engaging your core during exercises like squats, lunges, and even while walking or running.

- **Practice Pilates and Yoga:** These disciplines are excellent for building core strength and stability, emphasizing controlled movements, breathing, and mindfulness.

Safe and Effective Core Training

- **Warm-Up Properly:** Start with a light warm-up to get your blood flowing and prepare your muscles for exercise, reducing the risk of injury.
- **Prioritize Form Over Quantity:** Ensure you're performing each exercise with proper form. It's better to do fewer repetitions correctly than many with poor form, which can lead to strain or injury.
- **Progress Gradually:** Begin with basic core exercises, and as your strength improves, gradually increase the intensity and complexity of your workouts.

. . .

Listening to Your Body

• **Be Mindful of Back Pain:** While core exercises can help alleviate back pain over time, it's important to avoid any movements that cause discomfort or pain in your back. If an exercise feels wrong, stop and seek advice from a fitness professional.

• **Balance Core Workouts:** Just like any other muscle group, the core needs time to recover. Ensure you're not overtraining by incorporating rest days into your fitness regimen.

Incorporating Core Stability into Daily Life

• **Mindful Movement:** Practice engaging your core during everyday activities. Whether you're sitting, standing, or bending, a little mindfulness can go a long way in reinforcing core engagement.

• **Breathing Techniques:** Learning to breathe properly, particularly diaphragmatic breathing, can also engage and strengthen the core, supporting stability and overall health.

. . .

Core stability is the cornerstone of a strong, functional body, especially as we navigate the challenges and changes that come with age. By incorporating core strengthening into your fitness routine, you'll build a solid foundation that supports all other aspects of physical health and activity.

PART III

NUTRITION AND HYDRATION

9

NUTRITION AND HYDRATION: EATING FOR ENERGY

Nutrition plays a crucial role in providing the energy necessary for daily activities and exercise. After forty, the body's metabolism changes, and maintaining energy levels becomes a key concern. Understanding how to fuel your body can help you feel more vibrant and energized throughout the day.

The Basics of Energy Nutrition

- **Balanced Diet:** Focus on a diet that incorporates a variety of nutrients. Aim for a mix of carbohydrates, proteins, and fats to ensure a steady supply of energy.

• **Carbohydrates:** Opt for complex carbohydrates like whole grains, vegetables, and fruits, which provide a slow and steady release of energy.

• **Proteins:** Include lean sources of protein such as chicken, fish, tofu, legumes, and eggs to support muscle repair and growth.

• **Healthy Fats:** Incorporate sources of healthy fats like avocados, nuts, seeds, and olive oil, which are essential for hormone production and nutrient absorption.

Timing Your Meals

• **Regular Meals and Snacks:** Eating at regular intervals helps maintain blood sugar levels, preventing energy dips. Aim for three balanced meals and one to two healthy snacks per day.

• **Pre- and Post-Workout Nutrition:** Fuel your body with a light, carbohydrate-rich snack before exercise for immediate energy. Following your workout, consume a combination of carbohydrates and protein to replenish energy stores and aid muscle recovery.

. . .

Hydration and Energy

- **Stay Hydrated:** Water is essential for optimal energy levels. Even mild dehydration can lead to fatigue and decreased performance. Aim to drink at least 8 cups (64 ounces) of water daily, and more if you're active or in a hot environment.

Micronutrients for Energy

- **Vitamins and Minerals:** Ensure your diet includes foods rich in vitamins and minerals that play a role in energy production, such as B vitamins, iron, magnesium, and vitamin D. Leafy greens, nuts, seeds, dairy, and fortified foods are good sources.

Energy-Sapping Foods to Avoid

. . .

- **Limit Sugar and Processed Foods:** While sugary and highly processed foods can provide a quick energy boost, they often lead to a rapid crash. Limit these foods and opt for whole, nutrient-dense options instead.

Listening to Your Body

- **Mindful Eating:** Pay attention to how different foods affect your energy levels and overall wellbeing. Use this awareness to make informed choices about your diet.

Adapting to Your Needs

- **Personalized Nutrition:** Recognize that nutritional needs vary from person to person. Consider consulting a registered dietitian for personalized advice, especially if you have specific health conditions or dietary restrictions.

. . .

Eating for energy involves more than just consuming calories; it's about choosing the right types of foods at the right times to sustain your energy levels and support your fitness goals. By understanding and applying these principles, you can fuel your body effectively, enhancing your overall vitality and performance.

10

NUTRITION AND HYDRATION: HYDRATION

Water plays myriad vital roles in the body, from regulating body temperature and maintaining blood volume to facilitating cellular functions and aiding in digestion. As we age, staying adequately hydrated becomes even more critical, as dehydration can lead to a host of issues, including impaired physical performance, increased fatigue, and difficulty regulating body temperature.

The Importance of Staying Hydrated

- **Supports Physical Performance:** Adequate hydration is essential for maintaining endurance, strength, and power during physical activities. Even slight dehydration can significantly impact performance.

- **Enhances Energy Levels:** Proper hydration helps to ensure that nutrients are efficiently transported throughout the body, contributing to optimal energy production.
- **Promotes Cardiovascular Health:** Staying hydrated helps maintain blood volume, facilitating heart function and preventing excessive cardiovascular strain during exercise.
- **Aids in Recovery:** Adequate fluid intake is crucial for flushing out toxins and supporting muscle recovery post-exercise.

Recognizing Dehydration

Understanding the signs of dehydration can help you take proactive steps to rehydrate. Symptoms can include:

- Thirst
- Dry mouth
- Fatigue or dizziness

- Dark-colored urine
- Reduced urine output

How Much to Drink

- **General Guidelines:** While the "8 cups of water a day" rule is a good starting point, individual needs can vary based on factors such as age, weight, climate, and activity level. Aiming for pale yellow urine is a practical way to gauge hydration.
- **During Exercise:** Increase your water intake before, during, and after physical activity. A general recommendation is to drink 17-20 ounces of water 2-3 hours before exercising, 8 ounces during warm-up, 7-10 ounces every 10-20 minutes during exercise, and 8 ounces within 30 minutes after exercising.

Sources of Hydration

- **Water:** Plain water is the best way to hydrate. It's calorie-free, caffeine-free, and readily available.

• **Foods with High Water Content:** Incorporating fruits and vegetables with high water content, such as cucumbers, lettuce, watermelon, and strawberries, can also contribute to overall hydration.

• **Other Beverages:** Herbal teas, milk, and juice can contribute to your daily fluid intake but be mindful of calorie content and additives in some beverages.

Monitoring Your Hydration

• **Listen to Your Body:** Thirst is a clear signal that your body needs fluids, but don't wait until you're thirsty to drink. Regularly sipping water throughout the day is key.

• **Monitor Urine Color:** Use the color of your urine as a guide to your hydration status. Aim for pale, straw-colored urine as an indication of proper hydration.

Hydration Strategies

. . .

- **Carry a Water Bottle:** Having a water bottle on hand encourages regular sipping, making it easier to meet your hydration needs.
- **Set Reminders:** Setting reminders on your phone or computer can prompt you to take hydration breaks, ensuring consistent intake throughout the day.

Proper hydration is a cornerstone of health and an essential part of any fitness regimen, especially for individuals over forty. By understanding the importance of hydration, recognizing the signs of dehydration, and employing effective strategies to maintain hydration, you can support your body's needs and enhance your overall fitness and wellbeing.

11

NUTRITION AND HYDRATION: SUPPLEMENTS

While a balanced diet should always be the first priority for meeting nutritional needs, supplements can play a supportive role in filling nutritional gaps, enhancing performance, and supporting overall health. For those over forty, certain supplements may be particularly beneficial, given the changes in metabolism, bone density, and muscle mass associated with aging.

Understanding Supplements

- **Purpose:** Supplements are intended to complement the diet, not replace it. They can provide vitamins, minerals, and other nutrients in concentrated form.

• **Types:** There's a wide range of supplements available, including multivitamins, mineral supplements, omega-3 fatty acids, protein powders, and specialized supplements like glucosamine, probiotics, and antioxidants.

Key Supplements for Over Forty

• **Multivitamins:** A daily multivitamin can help fill nutritional gaps, especially if your diet lacks variety or you're avoiding certain food groups.

• **Vitamin D and Calcium:** These are crucial for bone health, which becomes a concern with increasing age. Vitamin D is also essential for immune function and may help with mood regulation.

• **Omega-3 Fatty Acids:** Found in fish oil supplements, omega-3s are known for their anti-inflammatory properties and benefits for heart and brain health.

• **Protein Supplements:** As muscle mass tends to decline with age, protein supplements can help meet increased protein needs, supporting muscle repair and growth.

- **Fiber Supplements:** With digestion slowing down in some individuals over forty, fiber supplements can aid in maintaining digestive health.

Considerations Before Taking Supplements

- **Consult Healthcare Providers:** Before starting any supplement regimen, it's crucial to consult with a healthcare provider, especially if you have underlying health conditions or are taking medications, as some supplements can interact with medications.
- **Quality Matters:** Not all supplements are created equal. Look for products that have been third-party tested for quality and purity.
- **Personalized Needs:** Consider your individual dietary restrictions, lifestyle, and specific health concerns when choosing supplements.

Managing Expectations

. . .

• **No Magic Solutions:** Supplements should not be seen as quick fixes for health and fitness goals. They work best when combined with a healthy diet, regular exercise, and a well-rounded lifestyle.

• **Ongoing Research:** The effectiveness and safety of many supplements continue to be studied. Stay informed about the latest research and adjust your supplement intake as needed.

The use of supplements can be a valuable addition to your nutrition and hydration strategy, particularly as you navigate the challenges of staying fit and healthy over forty. However, it's important to approach supplementation with informed caution, prioritizing a balanced diet and consulting with healthcare professionals to tailor a regimen that meets your specific needs.

PART IV

IMPORTANT LIFESTYLE FACTORS

12

LIFESTYLE FACTORS: SLEEP AND RECOVERY

Adequate sleep and proper recovery are not merely adjuncts to a fitness regimen; they are foundational elements of overall health and wellbeing. As we age, the body's recovery processes can slow down, making it even more crucial to prioritize restorative practices.

The Importance of Sleep

- **Physical Repair:** During sleep, the body undergoes significant repair and regeneration processes, including muscle repair, tissue growth, and hormone synthesis, which are vital for fitness recovery.

• **Cognitive Function:** Quality sleep is essential for cognitive functions such as memory, focus, and decision-making, impacting daily performance and overall quality of life.

• **Emotional Wellbeing:** Sleep has a profound impact on mood and emotional resilience, helping to manage stress and reduce the risk of depression and anxiety.

Optimizing Sleep Quality

• **Regular Sleep Schedule:** Aim to go to bed and wake up at the same time every day to regulate your body's internal clock, enhancing sleep quality.

• **Sleep-Inducing Environment:** Create a sleep-friendly environment that is dark, quiet, and cool. Consider using blackout curtains, white noise machines, and comfortable bedding to promote uninterrupted sleep.

• **Pre-Bedtime Routine:** Establish a calming pre-sleep routine to signal to your body that it's time to wind down. Activities might include reading, taking a warm bath, or practicing relaxation exercises like deep breathing or meditation.

Recovery Strategies

- **Active Recovery:** Incorporate light, restorative activities on rest days, such as walking, gentle yoga, or stretching, to promote circulation and aid muscle recovery.
- **Rest Days:** Schedule regular rest days into your fitness regimen to allow your body time to recover and prevent overtraining.
- **Hydration and Nutrition:** Adequate hydration and nutrition play crucial roles in recovery. Ensure you're replenishing fluids and nutrients lost during exercise, focusing on a balanced intake of carbohydrates, proteins, and healthy fats.

Managing Recovery as You Age

. . .

• **Listen to Your Body:** Be mindful of your body's signals and allow for additional recovery time if needed. Recovery rates can vary widely among individuals and may change as you age.

• **Incorporate Recovery Tools:** Consider using tools such as foam rollers, massage balls, or even professional massage therapy to aid in muscle recovery and reduce soreness.

• **Balance Intensity:** Adjust the intensity and volume of your workouts to match your body's recovery capacity, ensuring a balance that promotes fitness gains without overtaxing the body.

Prioritizing sleep and recovery is essential for sustaining fitness, health, and wellbeing, especially over forty. By implementing strategies to enhance sleep quality and ensuring adequate recovery time, you can support your body's natural repair processes, improve fitness outcomes, and maintain a high quality of life.

13

LIFESTYLE FACTORS: STRESS MANAGEMENT

Stress is an inevitable part of life, but its management is crucial, especially as we navigate the complexities of life over forty. Chronic stress can lead to a host of health issues, including hypertension, weakened immune function, and increased risk of chronic diseases, not to mention its impact on mood, motivation, and overall quality of life.

Understanding the Impact of Stress

- **Physical Health:** Chronic stress can contribute to a range of health problems, from cardiovascular disease to digestive issues, and can impair recovery and performance in fitness activities.

• **Mental Wellbeing:** High stress levels can affect cognitive functions, such as concentration and memory, and can lead to anxiety, depression, and sleep disturbances.

Effective Stress Management Techniques

• **Regular Physical Activity:** Exercise itself is a powerful stress reliever. It releases endorphins, the body's natural mood elevators, and can help reduce anxiety and improve sleep.

• **Mindfulness and Meditation:** Practices like mindfulness, meditation, and deep-breathing exercises can significantly reduce stress levels, enhance emotional balance, and improve overall mental health.

• **Adequate Rest and Relaxation:** Ensuring sufficient downtime and engaging in activities you enjoy can help recharge your batteries and reduce stress. This could include hobbies, spending time with loved ones, or simply taking moments of quiet solitude.

. . .

Time Management

• **Prioritize and Organize:** Effective time management can alleviate the stress of feeling overwhelmed. Prioritize tasks, delegate when possible, and set realistic deadlines.

• **Learn to Say No:** Recognizing your limits and saying no to additional responsibilities can help maintain a manageable workload and reduce stress.

Social Support

• **Seek Support:** Sharing your concerns and experiences with friends, family, or a support group can provide emotional relief and valuable perspectives on managing stress.

• **Professional Help:** If stress becomes overwhelming, consider seeking help from a mental health professional who can provide coping strategies and therapeutic support.

. . .

Lifestyle Adjustments

- **Healthy Diet:** Nutrition plays a role in stress management. A balanced diet can help stabilize mood and energy levels.
- **Sleep Hygiene:** As mentioned earlier, quality sleep is crucial for stress management and overall wellbeing.

Coping Strategies

- **Adaptive Coping:** Develop adaptive coping strategies that address the cause of stress and lead to constructive solutions, rather than relying on avoidance or substance use.
- **Relaxation Techniques:** Incorporate relaxation techniques into your daily routine, such as yoga, progressive muscle relaxation, or guided imagery, to help unwind and destress.

. . .

Effectively managing stress is a vital component of maintaining health and fitness, particularly for those over forty. By implementing a range of stress management techniques and making lifestyle adjustments, you can enhance your capacity to cope with stress, improve your physical and mental health, and support your fitness goals.

14

LIFESTYLE FACTORS: TIME MANAGEMENT

Good time management is key to maintaining a healthy lifestyle and achieving fitness goals. It involves planning and controlling how much time to spend on specific activities, enhancing productivity, and reducing stress. For individuals over forty, who often juggle multiple responsibilities, mastering time management can be particularly transformative.

Recognizing Time Constraints

- **Audit Your Time:** Keep a record of your daily activities for a week to identify where your time goes.

This can help pinpoint areas where you can gain time for fitness and other health-promoting activities.

• **Set Priorities:** Determine what's most important to you and what aligns with your long-term health and fitness goals. This might mean re-evaluating less essential activities that consume significant time.

Effective Planning

• **Weekly Planning:** At the start of each week, map out your schedule, including work commitments, family activities, and fitness sessions. This visual overview can help you find balance and ensure you're allocating time for your priorities.

• **Daily To-Do Lists:** Break down your weekly plan into daily tasks. A to-do list can keep you focused and provide a sense of accomplishment as you tick off completed items.

Integrating Fitness into Your Schedule

. . .

• **Flexible Fitness:** Choose fitness activities that fit easily into your life. Short, home-based workouts can sometimes be more practical than traveling to a gym.

• **Active Commuting:** If possible, incorporate physical activity into your commute, such as walking, cycling, or using public transport that involves some walking.

• **Exercise Snacking:** Consider short bouts of exercise spread throughout the day, such as a 10-minute walk in the morning, a quick midday body-weight circuit, and an evening stretching session.

Utilizing Technology

• **Fitness Apps:** Use apps to plan workouts, track progress, get new ideas, simplify your workload and planning, and even squeeze in short exercise sessions guided by virtual trainers.

• **Calendar Apps:** Digital calendars can be powerful tools for time management, allowing you to set reminders for workouts, meal prep, and relaxation time.

. . .

Delegation and Saying No

• **Delegate Tasks:** Share responsibilities at home and work when possible to free up time for health-promoting activities.

• **Learn to Say No:** Politely declining additional commitments that don't align with your priorities can help preserve your time for essential activities, including fitness and recovery.

Balance and Flexibility

• **Be Flexible:** Life is unpredictable. Be prepared to adjust your plans as needed while staying focused on your overall goals.

• **Avoid Perfectionism:** Striving for perfection in every task can be counterproductive. Sometimes, 'good enough' is sufficient, freeing up more time for your priorities.

. . .

Mastering time management is a critical skill that can significantly enhance your ability to maintain a balanced lifestyle and achieve your fitness goals. By strategically planning and prioritizing your time, you can ensure that health and fitness remain integral parts of your daily life, regardless of other commitments.

PART V

INJURY PREVENTION AND MANAGEMENT

15

INJURY PREVENTION AND MANAGEMENT: COMMON OVER-40 INJURIES

Recognizing the most prevalent injuries that occur over the age of forty is the first step in prevention and management. This awareness allows for the adoption of targeted strategies to reduce the risk of these injuries and ensure a more sustainable approach to fitness and daily activities.

1. Rotator Cuff Injuries

- **Overview:** The rotator cuff is a group of muscles and tendons that stabilize the shoulder. Injuries here can range from inflammation (tendinitis) to tears, often resulting from repetitive overhead movements or wear over time.

• **Prevention:** Strengthening the shoulder muscles, improving flexibility, and avoiding repetitive overhead activities can help prevent rotator cuff injuries. Incorporating exercises that target the rotator cuff and surrounding muscles into your fitness regimen is beneficial.

2. Lower Back Pain

• **Overview:** Lower back pain can result from a variety of factors, including poor posture, weak core muscles, and degenerative changes in the spine. It's one of the most common complaints among adults over forty.

• **Prevention:** Maintaining a strong core, practicing good posture, and incorporating flexibility exercises, particularly for the hips and hamstrings, can significantly reduce the risk of lower back pain. It's also important to use proper form when lifting and to avoid prolonged sitting.

3. Knee Injuries

• **Overview:** The knees can suffer from osteoarthritis, tendinitis, and meniscus tears, often exacerbated by excess weight, previous injuries, and wear and tear from high-impact activities.

• **Prevention:** Strengthening the muscles around the knees, including the quadriceps, hamstrings, and calves, can help stabilize the knee joint. Low-impact exercises, such as cycling or swimming, can maintain fitness while minimizing stress on the knees.

4. Achilles Tendinitis

• **Overview:** This injury involves inflammation of the Achilles tendon, the large tendon connecting the calf muscles to the heel. It often results from sudden increases in activity level, tight calf muscles, or improper footwear.

• **Prevention:** Gradual progression in activity intensity, regular calf and Achilles stretching, and wearing supportive footwear can help prevent this condition.

5. Plantar Fasciitis

• **Overview:** Characterized by pain in the bottom of the foot, particularly near the heel, this condition results from inflammation of the plantar fascia, a thick band of tissue that runs across the bottom of your foot.

- **Prevention:** Maintaining a healthy weight, wearing supportive shoes, and stretching the feet and calf muscles can reduce the risk of plantar fasciitis.

Understanding these common injuries and their prevention strategies is crucial for maintaining an active and healthy lifestyle over forty. By incorporating targeted exercises, practicing good form, building strength and flexibility, and listening to your body, you can significantly reduce the risk of these common issues and continue to enjoy a wide range of physical activities.

16

INJURY PREVENTION AND MANAGEMENT: WHEN TO REST VS. WHEN TO PUSH

Balancing the fine line between pushing your limits for fitness gains and resting for recovery and injury prevention is an art that becomes increasingly important as we age. Understanding the difference between good pain (associated with muscle growth and endurance building) and bad pain (indicating potential injury) is key.

Listening to Your Body

• **Good Pain vs. Bad Pain:** Good pain, such as the mild, achy soreness after a challenging workout (delayed onset muscle soreness), is normal and a sign of muscle adaptation. Bad pain, however, is sharp, acute, or persistent, signaling possible injury or overtraining.

- **Fatigue and Performance:** Pay attention to overall levels of fatigue and performance during workouts. A general feeling of tiredness and decreased performance could indicate the need for rest and recovery.

Recognizing Overtraining

- **Symptoms of Overtraining:** Symptoms can include excessive fatigue, declining performance, sleep disturbances, increased susceptibility to colds and infections, and persistent muscle or joint soreness.
- **Response to Overtraining:** If you suspect overtraining, allow more time for rest and recovery. Consider reducing the intensity and volume of your workouts for a period to allow your body to recuperate.

The Role of Rest and Recovery

. . .

• **Scheduled Rest Days:** Incorporate regular rest days into your fitness regimen to allow your body time to recover. These days are crucial for muscle repair, strength building, and injury prevention.

• **Active Recovery:** Engage in low-intensity, restorative activities such as walking, gentle yoga, or stretching on rest days. Active recovery can aid circulation and facilitate the healing process without putting undue stress on the body.

Mental and Emotional Signs

• **Motivation and Mood:** A significant drop in motivation or a persistent negative mood related to exercise can be a sign that your body and mind need a break. Rest and engage in activities that rejuvenate your mental and emotional energy.

• **Stress and Sleep:** High stress levels and poor sleep quality can impair recovery. If stress and sleep issues are affecting your fitness routine, it may be time to prioritize stress management techniques and sleep hygiene.

. . .

Making Informed Decisions

- **Err on the Side of Caution:** If in doubt, choose rest over pushing through potential pain or fatigue. It's better to take a short break now than to risk an injury that could set you back weeks or months.
- **Consult Professionals:** When dealing with persistent pain or discomfort, seek advice from healthcare or fitness professionals to get an accurate assessment and guidance.

Navigating the balance between pushing your limits and resting is critical for long-term fitness and health, especially as the body ages. By tuning into your body's signals, recognizing the signs of overtraining, and appreciating the value of rest and recovery, you can maintain a healthy and sustainable fitness regimen.

17

INJURY PREVENTION AND MANAGEMENT: WORKING WITH HEALTH PROFESSIONALS

Engaging with healthcare and fitness professionals is a crucial step in preventing injuries, managing existing conditions, and optimizing overall fitness, especially as we age. Professionals can offer tailored advice, therapeutic interventions, and guidance based on the latest research and clinical expertise.

The Value of Professional Guidance

- **Preventive Care:** Regular check-ups with a healthcare provider can help identify risk factors for injuries or chronic conditions before they become problematic. Early intervention can prevent minor issues from escalating into more serious injuries.

• **Accurate Diagnosis:** Should an injury occur, healthcare professionals can provide an accurate diagnosis, which is essential for effective treatment. Self-diagnosis and treatment can lead to prolonged recovery or further injury.

• **Tailored Treatment Plans:** Based on your specific condition, health professionals can develop personalized treatment plans that may include physical therapy, medication, exercise modifications, or, in some cases, surgical intervention.

Types of Health Professionals

• **Primary Care Physicians:** Your primary doctor can offer initial advice on injury prevention and management and refer you to specialists as needed.

• **Physical Therapists:** Specializing in movement and function, physical therapists can develop rehabilitation programs to recover from injuries, improve mobility, and prevent future injuries.

• **Sports Medicine Specialists:** These physicians are trained to address physical fitness, preventive care, and the treatment of injuries related to sports and exercise.

- **Certified Fitness Trainers:** Trainers with certifications in corrective exercise or who have experience working with older adults can design fitness programs that accommodate and prevent injuries.

Building a Support Team

- **Communication:** Keep open lines of communication with your healthcare and fitness professionals, sharing your goals, concerns, and any changes in your condition.
- **Collaboration:** Work collaboratively with your team, providing feedback on what is or isn't working, to adjust your treatment and fitness plan as needed.

Navigating Healthcare

. . .

- **Insurance and Costs:** Understand your health insurance coverage and any out-of-pocket costs associated with treatment or consultations. Some preventive and rehabilitative services may be covered under your plan.
- **Seeking Second Opinions:** If recommended treatments don't align with your goals or if you're unsure about a diagnosis, seeking a second opinion can provide additional perspectives and options.

Leveraging the expertise of health and fitness professionals not only aids in the prevention and management of injuries but also in optimizing your overall health and fitness strategy. This collaborative approach ensures that your activities are both safe and effective, allowing you to maintain an active lifestyle at any age.

PART VI

STAYING MOTIVATED

18

STAYING MOTIVATED: COMMUNITY AND SUPPORT

Our goal of maintaining fitness and health, particularly as we age, does not need to be undertaken alone. The support of a community, whether it's family, friends, or like-minded individuals, can be a powerful motivator, helping to keep you engaged, committed, and inspired.

The Power of Social Support

- **Accountability:** Having someone to share your goals with can significantly increase your accountability. Whether it's a workout buddy, a group class, or an online community, knowing others are invested in your success can motivate you to stay on track.

• **Shared Experiences:** Engaging with others who are on similar journeys can provide a sense of camaraderie. Sharing challenges, successes, and tips can make the process more enjoyable and less daunting.

• **Encouragement:** During times of struggle or when motivation wanes, a supportive community can offer the encouragement needed to push through. Positive reinforcement from others can reignite your drive and commitment.

Building Your Support Network

• **Join Fitness Groups or Clubs:** Look for local running, cycling, or walking groups. Many communities have groups for various levels of fitness and interests.

• **Explore Group Fitness Classes:** Group classes, whether in-person or virtual, can provide structure, variety, and a built-in community of individuals with similar goals.

• **Engage in Online Communities:** Online forums, social media groups, and fitness apps can connect you with a broader community. These platforms often offer the opportunity to share progress, challenges, and encouragement.

- **Participate in Events:** Joining fitness challenges, races, or charity events can connect you with others and add a motivational goal to your fitness journey.

Leveraging Family and Friends

- **Involve Your Loved Ones:** Share your fitness goals with family and friends. They can provide emotional support and may even join you in your activities, creating shared experiences and memories.
- **Set Group Goals:** Setting a collective health or fitness goal with friends or family can be a fun way to stay motivated and accountable.

The Role of Professional Support

. . .

- **Work with a Trainer or Coach:** A professional can offer not only expertise but also motivational support. They can tailor your program to your needs, making adjustments as you progress, and celebrate your achievements with you.
- **Seek Health Coaching:** For broader lifestyle changes, a health coach can offer guidance, accountability, and support, helping you to navigate challenges and stay focused on your goals.

The impact of community and support in maintaining motivation cannot be overstated. By building a network of support and engaging with a community, you can enhance your fitness journey, making it more enjoyable, sustainable, and successful.

19

STAYING MOTIVATED: TRACKING PROGRESS

Monitoring your fitness journey not only helps in staying motivated but also in adjusting your goals and strategies as needed. Seeing improvements, no matter how small, can be a powerful motivator and a reminder of why you started.

Why Track Your Progress?

- **Measurable Outcomes:** Tracking provides quantifiable data on your improvements, whether it's increased strength, improved endurance, weight loss, or reduced medication dependency.

- **Goal Reassessment:** Regularly reviewing your progress helps in reassessing and setting new goals, keeping your fitness journey aligned with your current capabilities and aspirations.
- **Motivation Boost:** Reflecting on how far you've come can be a significant motivational boost, especially during periods of plateau or decreased motivation.

Effective Ways to Track Progress

- **Fitness Journals or Apps:** Documenting your workouts, dietary habits, and how you feel each day can provide insights into your progress and the effectiveness of your regimen.
- **Wearable Fitness Trackers:** Devices that track steps, heart rate, sleep patterns, and workout intensity can offer a detailed overview of your daily activity levels and health metrics.
- **Photos and Measurements:** Taking regular photos and measurements (such as weight, waist circumference, or body fat percentage) can visually document changes over time.

- **Performance Benchmarks:** Setting and tracking performance-related goals, such as running a certain distance, achieving a personal best in lifting, or completing a set number of push-ups, can be highly motivating.

Celebrating Milestones

- **Set Milestone Goals:** Break down your long-term goals into smaller milestones, making them more manageable and less daunting.
- **Celebrate Achievements:** Each time you reach a milestone, celebrate your success. This could be through a small reward, sharing your achievement with your support network, or simply taking a moment to reflect on your accomplishment.

Reflective Practice

- **Regular Review Sessions:** Set aside time weekly or monthly to review your progress. Reflect on what's working, what isn't, and any adjustments needed to keep moving forward.

- **Learn from Setbacks:** Use setbacks or plateaus as learning opportunities. Reflecting on challenges and how you overcame them can be a source of motivation and a guide for future strategies.

Tracking your progress is a fundamental component of staying motivated and committed to your fitness journey. It allows you to see the tangible results of your efforts, reassess and adjust your goals, and celebrate the milestones along the way.

20

STAYING MOTIVATED: ADAPTING OVER TIME

Change is an inherent part of life and your fitness journey. Recognizing and embracing the need for adaptation ensures that your fitness regimen remains relevant, enjoyable, and effective, even as your circumstances, capabilities, and goals evolve over time.

Recognizing the Need for Change

- **Physical Changes:** As we age, changes in physical capabilities, recovery times, and injury risks may necessitate adjustments in the intensity, type, and frequency of exercises.

- **Lifestyle Shifts:** Changes in job responsibilities, family dynamics, or living situations can impact available time for fitness activities, requiring adaptations in your routine.
- **Evolving Goals:** Your initial fitness goals may transform as you progress. What started as a weight loss journey might evolve into a focus on strength training, flexibility, or endurance.

Strategies for Effective Adaptation

- **Stay Informed:** Keep abreast of the latest fitness research and trends, especially those relevant to your age group. This knowledge can inform adjustments to your routine.
- **Seek Professional Advice:** Regular consultations with fitness professionals can provide personalized insights into how best to adapt your routine to suit your changing needs.
- **Incorporate Variety:** Introducing new activities or varying your routine can not only accommodate physical and lifestyle changes but also prevent boredom and reinvigorate your motivation.

• **Listen to Your Body:** Pay attention to your body's signals. Increased discomfort, a plateau in progress, or decreased enthusiasm for your current routine are all cues that it might be time to make some changes.

Embracing New Challenges

• **Set New Goals:** As you achieve your initial goals, set new ones to keep challenging yourself. These should be realistic, considering your current situation, but ambitious enough to push you forward.

• **Learn New Skills:** Taking up a new sport or fitness activity can rekindle your interest and motivation. Whether it's learning to swim, taking up cycling, or joining a dance class, new skills can offer fresh challenges and rewards.

Maintaining Flexibility in Your Approach

. . .

- **Be Open to Change:** View your fitness journey as a dynamic, evolving process. Being open to change can help you stay aligned with your current abilities and life circumstances.
- **Balance Is Key:** Strive for a balanced approach that incorporates cardiovascular health, strength, flexibility, and mental wellbeing, adjusting the focus as needed over time.

Adapting your fitness journey over time is not a sign of setback but a strategy for sustainable success and fulfillment. By staying flexible, embracing new challenges, and making informed adjustments, you can maintain motivation and continue to thrive in your fitness endeavors, regardless of age or changing circumstances.

CONCLUSION: THE LONG-TERM JOURNEY

As we wrap up this guidebook, it's crucial to recognize that achieving and maintaining fitness over forty is not just a goal but a continuous journey. This path is as much about the steps along the way as it is about the milestones achieved. Embracing this journey with patience, resilience, and a positive mindset can lead to a fulfilling and vibrant life.

Embracing a Holistic Approach

Your fitness journey is not solely about physical accomplishments but also about nurturing your mental, emotional, and social wellbeing. Integrating aspects of nutrition, rest, stress management, and community into your routine is vital for a balanced and holistic approach to health.

The Power of Consistency

Consistency is the cornerstone of success in any fitness journey. Small, daily efforts accumulate over time, leading to significant long-term results. It's the regularity of your actions, rather than their scale, that makes the most profound impact.

Adapting to Life's Changes

Life is dynamic, filled with changes and unexpected turns. Adapting your fitness goals and methods to align with your evolving needs and circumstances is not only practical but essential for long-term success. Stay flexible, open to learning, and ready to adjust your sails to the changing winds.

. . .

Celebrating Every Step

Each step forward, no matter how small, is a victory in the journey of fitness and health. Celebrate your progress, learn from setbacks, and recognize that every effort contributes to your overall wellbeing. Acknowledge your achievements, both big and small, and let them fuel your motivation to continue.

Cultivating Self-Compassion

Be kind to yourself on this journey. There will be days of high energy and triumph, but also days when motivation wanes or life gets in the way. Treat yourself with compassion and understanding, recognizing that rest and recovery are just as important as the workouts themselves.

A Lifelong Commitment

. . .

Finally, view your fitness journey as a lifelong commitment to yourself. It's a pledge to care for your body, mind, and spirit, embracing each day with the intention to live fully and healthily. This journey is uniquely yours, enriched by your experiences, challenges, and triumphs.

As we conclude this guidebook, remember that the pursuit of fitness, health, and wellbeing over forty is a rewarding journey that enhances every aspect of your life. Stay committed, be adaptable, and cherish the journey, for it is in the journey that life's true richness is found.

PART VII

APPENDICES

21

APPENDIX: GLOSSARY OF TERMS AND KEY CONCEPTS

Aerobic Exercise

Physical activity that relies on the oxygen in muscles to generate energy, typically involving moderate-intensity, sustained exercise such as jogging, cycling, or swimming.

Body Composition

The ratio of different types of body tissues, primarily fat mass and lean mass, including muscles, bones, and organs.

Core Stability

The strength and coordination of the muscles surrounding the trunk and pelvis, which are crucial for maintaining balance, posture, and overall body strength.

Dynamic Stretching

A form of active movement that stretches the muscles to their full extent without holding the position, often used as part of a warm-up routine.

Flexibility

The ability of a joint to move through its complete range of motion and the elasticity of the muscles and tendons that surround the joint.

High-Intensity Interval Training (HIIT)

A training technique involving short bursts of intense exercise alternated with low-intensity recovery periods. It's known for its efficiency in improving fitness levels and burning calories.

Metabolism

The biochemical processes that occur within the body, converting food and drink into energy for both basic bodily functions and physical activity.

Overtraining

A condition resulting from excessive exercise without adequate rest, leading to decreased performance, fatigue, and increased risk of injury.

Progressive Muscle Relaxation

A technique for reducing stress and anxiety by tensing and then relaxing each muscle group in the body, promoting a sense of physical and mental relaxation.

Repetitions (Reps)

The number of times an exercise is performed continuously without rest. It's a key component of strength training routines.

Resistance Training

A type of physical activity that involves working against a force to increase muscle strength and endurance. Weights, resistance bands, and bodyweight exercises are common forms of resistance training.

Sarcopenia

The loss of skeletal muscle mass and strength associated with aging, which can affect balance, gait, and overall physical function.

Static Stretching

Stretching a muscle to its furthest point and then holding that position for a period of time, typically used to improve flexibility and cool down after exercise.

Tai Chi

A form of martial arts known for its gentle, flowing movements and deep breathing, often practiced for its health benefits, including stress reduction, balance improvement, and overall physical and mental wellbeing.

22

APPENDIX: RESOURCE LISTS AND RECOMMENDATIONS

Books

- *Younger Next Year: Live Strong, Fit, Sexy, and Smart —Until You're 80 and Beyond* by Chris Crowley and Henry S. Lodge, M.D.
- *The Blue Zones: 9 Lessons for Living Longer From the People Who've Lived the Longest* by Dan Buettner
- *Spark: The Revolutionary New Science of Exercise and the Brain* by John J. Ratey

Websites

. . .

• National Institute on Aging (www.nia.nih.gov): Offers a wealth of information on health and aging, including exercise tips and guidelines for older adults.

• American Council on Exercise (www.acefitness.org): Provides fitness resources, research, and certified professional directories.

• Mayo Clinic (www.mayoclinic.org): A comprehensive resource for health information, including articles on fitness and nutrition.

Apps

• MyFitnessPal: A comprehensive tool for tracking diet and exercise, helping users maintain or achieve their fitness and health goals.

• Strava: Ideal for tracking cycling and running workouts, offering community features to connect with other athletes.

• Headspace: Offers guided meditation and mindfulness practices, supporting mental health and stress management.

. . .

Professional Services

• Physical Therapists: Search for a licensed physical therapist through the American Physical Therapy Association's website (www.apta.org) to find professionals specializing in sports medicine or geriatric care.

• Certified Personal Trainers: Use the National Strength and Conditioning Association (www.nsca.com) or the American Council on Exercise (www.acefitness.org) to find certified trainers with experience in working with older adults.

• Registered Dietitians: The Academy of Nutrition and Dietetics (www.eatright.org) provides a directory to find dietitians specializing in various areas, including sports nutrition and wellness for older adults.

Online Communities and Forums

• Reddit Fitness (www.reddit.com/r/fitness): A community for fitness enthusiasts where you can find advice, motivation, and personal stories.

• Silver Sneakers (www.silversneakers.com):

Offers exercise programs for older adults, including a community forum for sharing experiences and support.

YouTube Channels

• Fitness Blender: Features a wide range of workout videos for different fitness levels and goals, including strength training, cardio, and flexibility.

• Yoga with Adriene: Offers yoga videos for all levels, focusing on mindfulness and physical wellbeing.

This resource list is intended to serve as a starting point, guiding you toward reliable and helpful information and support. As you continue on your fitness journey, you may discover many additional resources that resonate with your personal preferences and needs.

www.ingramcontent.com/pod-product-compliance
Lightning Source LLC
LaVergne TN
LVHW012109160826
845678LV00014B/3008